For my Mother and Father
and for Jerry Wexler

Schirmer Books
A Division of Macmillan, Inc.
866 Third Avenue, New York, N.Y. 10022

Collier Macmillan Canada, Inc.

Library of Congress Catalog Card Number: 83–16310

Printed in the United States of America

by Rapoport Printing Corporation

printing number
1 2 3 4 5 6 7 8 9 10

Library of Congress Cataloging in Publication Data

Friedman, Carol
  A moment's notice.

  Includes discographies and index.
  1. Jazz musicians – United States – Portraits.
I. Giddins, Gary. II. Title.
ML87.F84   1983   785.42'092'2 [B]   83–16310
ISBN 0-02-872040-7

GERRY MULLIGAN

Although Gerry Mulligan came of
musical age in the 1940s, and was a
primary architect of the cool school, his
style defies categorization. Born in New
York in 1927, Mulligan has the distinction
of being the only baritone saxophonist to
win a large popular following, a result of
his alluring sound, unperturbed sense
of time, and great melodic gift. He is
equally at home with traditional, swing,
and modern players, and his recording
partners have run the gamut from Ben
Webster to Charles Mingus. He first
attracted attention as an arranger for big
bands (Gene Krupa's and Claude
Thornhill's, among others) and Miles
Davis's nonet, but he became famous in
1952 when he introduced his pianoless
quartet. His front-line collaborators
included Chet Baker, Bob Brookmeyer,
and Art Farmer. Given his celebrity as
a soloist, it might seem quixotic of
Mulligan to struggle with a big band,
yet the splendid Concert Jazz Band,
which he's led on and off since 1960, is
very likely his greatest joy. *The Original
Gerry Mulligan Quartet* (Mosaic), *What
Is There to Say* (Columbia), *At the
Village Vanguard* (Verve), *Walk on the
Water* (DRG).

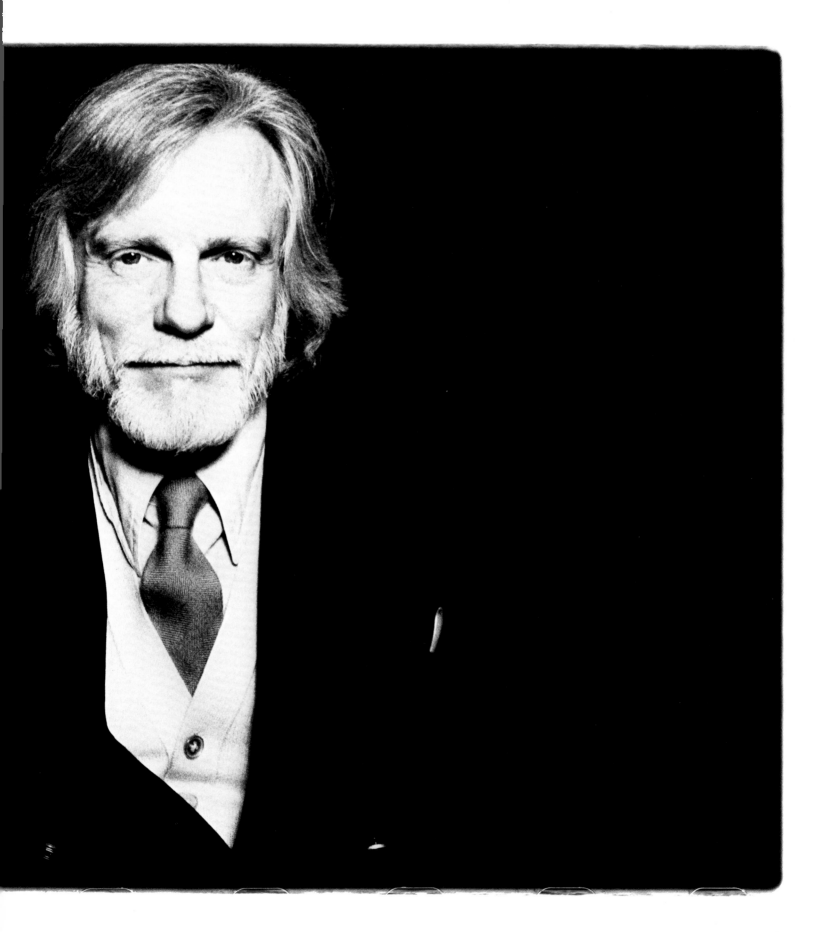

JOHNNY GRIFFIN

The fastest sax in the West, Johnny Griffin was originally influenced by what he calls the "sweetness and control" of Johnny Hodges and Ben Webster, but it was Charlie Parker who provided him with a stylistic model. Born in Chicago in 1928, he first won attention playing tenor duels with Arnett Cobb in Lionel Hampton's band. By the mid-1950s he was recognized as one of the most exciting saxophonists of his generation, soaring with Art Blakey's Jazz Messengers, replacing John Coltrane in Thelonious Monk's quartet, recording small combo and big band albums, and touring with fellow tenorist Eddie Lockjaw Davis. His solos often began with nervous fragments, which he juggled, preened, and accelerated into a blistering maze of arpeggios, trilled upper-register skeins, blues aphorisms, and hollers. In 1963 Griffin moved to Europe, where he began composing. He renewed his career in America with a series of successful tours beginning in 1978. *Blowin' Sessions* (Blue Note), *Thelonious Monk: At the Five Spot* (Milestone), *Change of Pace* (Riverside), *Return of the Phoenix* (Galaxy).

DEXTER GORDON

Tall, handsome, witty Dexter Gordon, with his unique broadsword of a tone and a penchant for unlikely melodic quotations, has a personal and musical charisma that magnetizes audiences. Born in Los Angeles in 1923, he combined the lithe, floating lyricism of Lester Young with the virile attack of Coleman Hawkins, and adapted the result to the complexities of bebop, providing an original foundation for the next generation of tenor saxophonists. In the early 1950s Gordon was famous chiefly for his thrilling tenor duels (his opponents over the years have included Wardell Gray, Teddy Edwards, Gene Ammons, Budd Johnson, Booker Ervin, and James Moody), but a decade later he emerged as a compelling interpreter of ballads. Dexter moved to Copenhagen in 1962, yet he kept up with stylistic developments, and his triumphant homecoming tour in 1976 boosted his popularity to new heights. *Long Tall Dexter* (Savoy), *Go!* (Blue Note), *Power!* (Prestige), *More Than You Know* (Steeple-Chase).

SNOOKY YOUNG

Eugene Edward "Snooky" Young, who has played with most of the major big bands of the past forty years, has been called the greatest lead trumpeter of all time. He manages to stamp brass sections with his own distinctive sound, displaying faultless precision and timing. Born in Dayton, Ohio, in 1919, Young made his mark with Jimmie Lunceford twenty years later. In the 1940s he played with Count Basie, Lionel Hampton, Les Hite, Benny Carter, and Gerald Wilson. He returned to Dayton for ten years and rejoined Basie in 1957. For the next five years, his dynamic phrasing helped shape the band's startling use of unison vibrato. Since 1962 Young has been on staff with the NBC studio orchestra, but his occasional appearances with smaller groups show that in addition to playing lead he can be a charming and provocative soloist. *Lunceford Special* (Columbia), *The Best of Count Basie* (Roulette), *The Boys from Dayton* (MJR), *Snooky and Marshall's Album* (Concord Jazz).

BETTY CARTER

Lille Mae Jones, born in Flint, Michigan, in 1930, was dubbed Betty "Be-Bop" Carter by Lionel Hampton after she joined his band at age 18. By then, she had already studied piano at the Detroit Conservatory and won an amateur show as a singer. After 30 months of singing and arranging with Hampton, her career proceeded slowly, notwithstanding associations with Miles Davis in 1958 (unrecorded), Ray Charles in 1961, and Sonny Rollins in 1963 (also unrecorded). Uncompromising and thoroughly committed to jazz, she became the object of a cult. After devoting most of the 1960s to her family, she re-emerged in the 1970s with a new authority, captivating audiences that forgot or never knew what jazz singing could be. Carter revitalizes standard songs with her sophisticated knowledge of harmony, profound understanding of lyrics, and uniquely sensuous voice. And when she can't find standard songs to make her point, she writes her own. *Ray Charles and Betty Carter* (ABC-Paramount), *What a Little Moonlight Can Do* (ABC-Impulse), *Finally* (Bush), *The Audience* (Bet-Car).

11

GRADY TATE

As the house drummer for Verve Records in the 1960s, Grady Tate earned a reputation as one of the most dependable drummers of the decade; his driving beat provided the foundation for numerous albums by Wes Montgomery, Stan Getz, Jimmy Smith, and Kenny Burrell, to name a few. His studio work led to extensive television appearances, including six years (1968–1974) with the *Tonight Show* orchestra. Born in Durham, North Carolina, in 1932, Tate played with Wild Bill Davis's band for two years before joining Quincy Jones's big band and gaining recognition as an all-around percussionist. Another career presented itself when he toured with Peggy Lee, who encouraged him to sing. During the 1970s he began singing more frequently, scoring a hit with "Windmills of My Mind." In recent years he has made drumming his priority once again, and is a stalwart presence at concerts and in recording studios. *Wes Montgomery: Movin' Wes* (Verve), *Jimmy Smith: Organ Grinder Swing* (Verve), *Stan Getz: Sweet Rain* (Verve), *Windmills of My Mind* (Skye).

WALT BOLDEN

Born in Hartford, Connecticut, in 1925, Walt Bolden was studying percussion at the Julius Hartt School of Music when he organized a trio with Horace Silver and bassist Joe Calloway. While passing through Hartford, Stan Getz hired the group as his rhythm section. An earthy bop drummer with swing roots, he moved to New York in 1953, and subsequently worked with Gerry Mulligan, Tony Scott, Coleman Hawkins, Howard McGhee, and Lambert, Hendricks & Ross. After a semi-sabbatical from music in the 1960s, Bolden became music director for Project Create in Harlem, conducting classes in musicianship, composition, and theory from 1973 to 1975. Two colleagues in the project, Harold Mabern and the late Wilbert Dyer, joined with him in the venture that signaled his official return to jazz: a 1978 album produced by his good friend, Grady Tate. *Stan Getz: A Pair of Kings* (Roost), *The Best of Lambert, Hendricks & Ross* (Columbia), *Walt Bolden* (Nemperor).

STAN GETZ

One of jazz's incorruptible romantics, Stan Getz was a prodigy of the 1940s. On the road at 15, he traveled with Jack Teagarden, Stan Kenton, Benny Goodman, and others before he turned 20, at which time he became famous as one of the original "Four Brothers" in Woody Herman's Second Herd. The ethereal timbre he demonstrated on Herman's "Early Autumn" was a benchmark of the cool school. Born in Philadelphia in 1927, Getz started on bass and bassoon before switching to the tenor saxophone. His distinctive sound, which can suggest icy detachment and searing intensity at the same time, was unmistakable, although he was strongly indebted to Lester Young and Dexter Gordon in his apprenticeship period. In the 1950s, despite illness and a long sojourn abroad, Getz emerged—along with Sonny Rollins and John Coltrane—as a major influence on tenor saxophonists. Beginning in 1962, he became something of a pop star with his Americanized bossa nova records; his brooding lyricism was perfectly matched to the melodies and rhythms of Brazil. Despite a brief flirtation with the accoutrements of fusion, he has continued to develop as a dramatic, swinging melodist, usually at the helm of a first-rate rhythm section. *Stan Getz* (Prestige), *Stan Getz and the Oscar Peterson Trio* (Verve), *Jazz Samba* (Verve), *Pure Getz* (Concord Jazz).

ORNETTE COLEMAN

The most paradoxical of musicians, Ornette Coleman is a determined radical who would like his music to be accepted by the masses. "Since America has 200 million people," he once said, "there is no survival problem for a person like myself because I am the only one doing what I do." The diversity of what this autodidactic saxophonist, composer, and theorist does is startling, ranging from free jazz (a term he coined) through a fully notated symphony to harmolodic funk (another Coleman term). Born in Fort Worth, Texas, in 1930, he began recording in Los Angeles in 1958; a year later, his quartet packed New York's Five Spot for six weeks. At the peak of his critical success, he took a sabbatical and never fully returned to a constant regimen of playing and recording. Whenever he did return to the jazz scene, he never failed to offer something new: he hired his nine-year-old son as drummer; performed on violin and trumpet; wrote a woodwind octet, a string quartet, and a symphony; and organized a unique jazz-funk band called Prime Time. Laconic and shy, possessor of an impressive art collection and an outrageous wardrobe, Coleman has brought into question every aspect of music (intonation, pitch, harmony, rhythm, melody), finding answers that are emotionally compelling and always surprising. *Free Jazz* (Atlantic), *At the Golden Circle, Vol. 1* (Blue Note), *Skies of America* (Columbia), *Of Human Feelings* (Antilles).

ED BLACKWELL

Ed Blackwell, one of the key innovators of free drumming, was born in New Orleans in 1927. When Ornette Coleman visited the city in 1947, they formed a musical partnership that would have profound consequences for jazz. Blackwell's ability to alter rhythms and displace accents in a way that negated traditional swing meter, while still providing a rocking foundation, made him the ideal percussionist for a music as anarchic yet fluid as Coleman's. A direct stylistic descendant of such pioneer New Orleans drummers as Baby Dodds and Zutty Singleton, he concentrated on the snares and toms rather than the cymbals. He also displayed a penchant for melodic African rhythms played with mallets. Although best known for his work with Coleman and Don Cherry, he has been heard with Eric Dolphy, Randy Weston, and others. The Coleman-inspired quartet Old and New Dreams is an ideal forum for his unmatched rhythmic jubilance. *Ornette!* (Atlantic), *The Great Concert of Eric Dolphy* (Prestige), *Mu* (BYG), *Old and New Dreams: Playing* (ECM)

CHARLIE HADEN

Charlie Haden was born in Iowa in 1937 to a family active in hillbilly music, which may account in part for the pastoral lyricism that informs his playing and composing. He brought his bass to California in the mid-1950s, about the same time that Ornette Coleman arrived, and was soon working with many of the important musicians in Los Angeles and San Francisco, including Art Pepper and Hampton Hawes. With Coleman he developed a style based more on melodic interaction than on harmonic accompaniment. Though originally associated with the avant-garde, he has proven himself at ease with every style of jazz, from Pee Wee Russell's to John McLaughlin's, always displaying empathy and tremendous warmth. The composer of several haunting melodies, Haden is best known for his collaborations with Coleman, Keith Jarrett, Old and New Dreams, and his own Liberation Music Orchestra. *Ornette Coleman: Change of the Century* (Atlantic), *Liberation Music Orchestra* (Impulse), *Closeness* (Horizon), *Old and New Dreams* (ECM).

DON CHERRY

Trumpeter Don Cherry was born in Oklahoma City in 1936, and met Ornette Coleman in California when he was 20. Playing a small brass instrument called the pocket trumpet, Cherry developed into an ideal foil for the saxophonist. Despite a relatively thin tone, his melodic inventiveness and total originality impressed many musicians (including Miles Davis), and he was soon participating in significant collaborations with John Coltrane, Sonny Rollins, and Albert Ayler. His technique increased considerably in the mid-1960s, when he began organizing his own groups. He displayed particular talent for extended compositions. More recently (especially since settling in Sweden in 1974), he added piano, flutes, exotic string instruments, and voice to his palette, revealing the increasing influence of Eastern music. Today, he's usually heard with Old and New Dreams, celebrating the legacy of Ornette Coleman. *Ornette on Tenor* (Atlantic), *Sonny Rollins: Our Man in Jazz* (RCA), *Symphony for Improvisors* (Blue Note), *Relativity Suite* (JCOA).

ART PEPPER

During his last years Art Pepper managed to convey through music the conviction that he'd been to hell and back. His playing had always been passionate, but in the classic recordings of the late 1950s, the intensity was lightened by a swinging, loping, bebopping proficiency. Then, after an uneasy period in which he sought to adapt the harshness of John Coltrane's tenor to the alto, he achieved the most ragingly expressionistic and poignant music of his beleaguered career—riddling tunes with stabbing phrases, keening tremolos, pitches just left of center, and unholy overtones. Pepper's hell was drug-induced. Born in Los Angeles in 1925, he attracted attention while touring with Stan Kenton in 1950, but just as his style was beginning to cohere, his life was disrupted by an addiction that sent him spinning in and out of jails and hospitals for nearly 20 years. After entering Synanon in 1969, where he met and married Laurie Miller, he began to put his music and life in order, publishing an autobiography *(Straight Life)* and recording prolifically. Pepper's music could be lovely and harrowing in the same phrase, and until his death in 1982, his live performances displayed the courage of a man living on borrowed time and determined to make the most of it. *Discoveries* (Savoy), *Art Pepper Meets the Rhythm Section* (Contemporary), *+11* (Contemporary), *Today* (Galaxy).

RON CARTER

Tall, lean, and quiet, Ron Carter is without a doubt the most famous and ubiquitous bassist of his generation, and so deft an accompanist that you're never quite sure whether he's being merely attentive or subtly running the show. Born in Ferndale, Michigan, in 1937, he earned degrees from the Eastman and Manhattan Schools of Music before freelancing with numerous jazz musicians, most notably Eric Dolphy, with whom he played cello as well as bass. Five years with Miles Davis (1963–1968) made his reputation; he was celebrated for his superb phrasing, intonation, and melodic agility. In 1973 he introduced the piccolo bass, a kind of cross between bass and cello, and, four years later, built a successful quartet around it. Though Carter is in constant demand for studio assignments, hardly a season goes by when he isn't playing duets in a New York club. *Eric Dolphy/Ron Carter: Magic* (Prestige), *Jim Hall/Ron Carter: Alone Together* (Milestone), *Piccolo* (Milestone), *Petrao* (Milestone).

FREDDIE HUBBARD

Freddie Hubbard was born to a musical family in Indianapolis in 1938. When he arrived in New York 20 years later, his technical brilliance and zeal established him almost immediately as a trumpeter for all seasons. He perfected his technique with J.J. Johnson, Sonny Rollins, and others before moving into the front line of the most propulsive hard-bop band of the period, Art Blakey's Jazz Messengers, for which he wrote several compositions. During those years, he also navigated the more adventurous charts of Eric Dolphy and Herbie Hancock, and lent his vibrant sound to avant-garde landmarks by Ornette Coleman and John Coltrane. Hailed for his versatility and the purity of his conception, Hubbard then took a left turn and made a series of commercial records often laden with strings and a disco beat. Despite tremendous popular success, he expressed discontent with those albums, and returned to recording jazz and touring with a quintet. His prodigious technique is still startling, and few musicians can generate as much excitement. *Art Blakey: Thermo* (Milestone), *Here to Stay* (Blue Note), *First Light* (CTI), *V.S.O.P.: The Quintet* (Columbia).

TONY BENNETT

Few singers can read a lyric as sensitively as Tony Bennett. In a style that
is emotionally direct and succinct, he is able to convey a song's meaning
with spontaneity and a sense of wonder. Born in Queens, New York, in 1926,
Bennett rose to fame with a string of pop hits beginning in 1950, among them
"Because of You" and "Rags to Riches." He fell out of favor at the height of rock
and roll, but scored a phenomenal comeback in 1962 with "I Left My Heart in San
Francisco." Frequent appearances on television helped to sustain a career that was
increasingly devoted to standards. Though not universally regarded as a jazz
singer, he is admired by numerous jazz enthusiasts and musicians, and has
performed with Duke Ellington, Count Basie, Woody Herman, Bobby Hackett,
Zoot Sims, and Bill Evans, among others. After more than 30 years, Bennett
remains one of the most widely respected interpreters of America's quality songs.
At Carnegie Hall (Columbia), *Let's Fall in Love* (Columbia), *The Tony Bennett–Bill
Evans Album* (Fantasy), *More Great Rodgers and Hart* (Improv).

◄ GEORGE COLEMAN

George Coleman's presence on a bandstand guarantees brawny, fiery, straight-ahead jazz. Born in Memphis in 1935, he played with several blues bands (including B.B. King's) before freelancing in Chicago and New York with such musicians as Ira Sullivan and John Gilmore. He recorded memorably with Max Roach in 1958, and toured for two years with Slide Hampton. His big break came in 1963–1964, when he took over the tenor chair in the Miles Davis Quintet, assuming a seat still warm from John Coltrane and Hank Mobley. After a brief spell in Europe, Coleman re-established himself in New York in the 1970s, playing with greater strength and conviction than ever. Some of his best work was with an ambitious, tightly arranged octet that, scandalously, has yet to be documented on American records.
Max Roach: Conversations (Milestone), *Herbie Hancock: Maiden Voyage* (Blue Note), *Cedar Walton: Eastern Rebellion* (Muse), *Meditation* (Timeless).

CECIL TAYLOR

For all the influences, jazz and classical, that have shaped his music, Cecil Taylor is a school unto himself. The first member of the avant-garde to record, he remains the most challenging musician of his generation—a herculean pianist of incredible stamina. Yet his music is hardly as monolithic as it sometimes seems to the novitiate; the nuance he achieves in his quiet moments is as exhilarating as the fearsome avalanches and jackhammer trills he creates by using the keyboard as a row of tuned drums. After a conservatory education, Taylor, who was born in New York in 1929, tested the jazz waters with such traditionalists as Johnny Hodges and Hot Lips Page. But he was uncomfortable in that milieu, and by 1956 he was leading a quartet that experimented with sheer energy as a substitute for countable time. Using a select group of musicians who have stayed with him for long periods (altoist Jimmy Lyons has been with Taylor's units for more than 20 years), he evolved a procedural method that he calls "unit structures." A student of dance, Taylor has collaborated in recent years with Mikhail Baryshnikov and Diane McIntyre.
In Transition (Blue Note), *Conquistador* (Blue Note), *Spring of Two Blue-J's* (Unit Core), *3 Phasis* (New World).

◄ LEE KONITZ

Lee Konitz was admired by musicians in the late 1940s as the one young alto saxophonist not entirely under the sway of Charlie Parker. Instead, he chose Lennie Tristano as his mentor and perfected an icily brilliant style that displayed unusual harmonic complexity while discarding obvious expressive effects. Born in Chicago in 1927, he recorded widely noted solos with Claude Thornhill, and subsequently took part in a couple of recording projects with Miles Davis. After a stay with Stan Kenton, his music became increasingly emotional as he opted for a more forceful sound and rhythmic approach. By the 1960s he made a point of playing with musicians from every era of jazz, employing a repertoire that encompassed transcriptions of Louis Armstrong and adaptations of Bartok, in settings that ranged from duets to large orchestra. He also pioneered the unaccompanied sax solo. In recent years, Konitz has led an ingenious nine-piece band. *Subconscious-Lee* (Prestige), *Motion* (Verve), *The Lee Konitz Duets* (Milestone), *Yes, Yes, Nonet* (SteepleChase).

GIL EVANS

WOODY SHAW

Born in North Carolina in 1944, Woody Shaw grew up in Newark, New Jersey, where his father sang with a gospel troupe called the Jubilee Singers. In high school he listened attentively to the trumpeters of the era, especially Booker Little and Freddie Hubbard, and at 18 he appeared on records with Eric Dolphy. After playing in Europe for a year (at the invitation of Dolphy, who died before Shaw arrived), he earned an enviable reputation as a sideman; his biting attack raised the energy level in bands led by Horace Silver, McCoy Tyner, Jackie McLean, Art Blakey, and others. Although he made his recorded debut as a leader in 1970, his real breakthrough came in 1976, when he participated in Dexter Gordon's homecoming quintet, led a seven-piece concert ensemble, and introduced a highly successful quintet that established him as a forceful trumpeter and bandleader. *Eric Dolphy: Iron Man* (Douglas), *Blackstone Legacy* (Contemporary), *Concert Ensemble* (Muse), *Master of the Art* (Musician).

WAYNE SHORTER

The career of Wayne Shorter, the most influential non–avant-garde tenor saxophonist to emerge in the 1960s, has consisted chiefly of three lengthy associations, each of which signaled a momentous change in his playing and composing styles. Born in Newark, New Jersey, in 1933, he first attracted attention with Art Blakey's Jazz Messengers (1959–1963) as a shrewd, fiercely swinging soloist somewhat under the spell of John Coltrane and Sonny Rollins. During six years with Miles Davis (1964–1970), he refined his tone and employed increasingly long, scalar, meditative phrases; similarly, his compositions – a staple of Davis's repertoire – became more complex and atmospheric. In 1971 Shorter joined with Joe Zawinul to create the most durable of all the jazz-rock collusions, Weather Report. Since that time he's played soprano as often as tenor, and his composing has reflected a growing interest in internationalism. Occasional appearances with V.S.O.P. as well as regular Weather Report tours affirm his stature as a major improvisor and composer. *Art Blakey: The Big Beat* (Blue Note), *Miles Davis: Miles Smiles* (Columbia), *Super Nova* (Blue Note), *Weather Report: 8:30* (Columbia).

MILT JACKSON

Milt Jackson brought the vibraharp into
modern jazz, broadening its emotional
and technical range, and enriching its
sound with a modulated vibrato. Born in
Detroit in 1923, he studied music at
Michigan State and was working in a
local group when Dizzy Gillespie
heard him and brought him to New York.
During the next few years, performing
with Thelonious Monk, Woody Herman,
and Tadd Dameron as well as Gillespie,
he became a major interpreter of
bop, turning the most sophisticated chord
progressions into extensions of the
blues. In 1952 he was the primary soloist
in the quartet that would evolve into the
Modern Jazz Quartet. During 22 years
with the MJQ his role became less
central and more integrated into the
multi-linear music of the group. The
composer of a classic blues, "Bag's
Groove," Jackson has long since
transcended any particular school of jazz;
he is beyond category—a natural.
Thelonius Monk: The Complete Genius
(Blue Note), *Modern Jazz Quartet*
(Prestige), *Big Band Bags* (Milestone),
Night Mist (Pablo).

IRA SULLIVAN

Ira Sullivan is the most highly esteemed multi-instrumentalist in jazz since Benny Carter. Not only does he switch effortlessly between brasses and reeds (finding time to play flute and drums as well) but he has a distinct style on each. Born to a musical family in Washington, D.C., in 1931, he was playing his father's trumpet at four and his mother's sax shortly afterward. Sullivan grew up in Chicago, where he gained prominence among the local modernists; as a member of the Bee Hive house band, he accompanied such visiting eminences as Charlie Parker and Lester Young. Yet, except for a brief tour with Art Blakey and occasional recordings (notably with Red Rodney, Billy Taylor, and Roland Kirk), he maintained a low profile. After moving to Florida in 1963, he emerged as a tireless force in the Miami jazz community. A series of recordings since 1975 and the organization of a quintet with Red Rodney in 1980 have brought him national recognition for the first time. *Ira Sullivan Quintet* (Delmark), *Ira Sullivan* (Horizon), *Peace* (Galaxy), *Sprint* (Musician).

RED RODNEY

Red Rodney has staged one of the more improbable comebacks of recent years. Born Robert Ronald Chudnik in Philadelphia in 1927, he first became known for his trumpet solos with the bands of Claude Thornhill, Gene Krupa, and Woody Herman. Originally a Harry James-influenced swing player, he switched his allegiance to bop after meeting Dizzy Gillespie, and in 1949 realized his dream of working with Charlie Parker. After eight months with Parker, winning recognition for his biting lyricism and attractive sound, Rodney should have been on the road to success. Instead, illness and a disordered personal life kept him in obscurity, playing in local groups and Las Vegas pit bands for more than 20 years. In 1974 he began to record and tour again, and five years later, playing with more fire than ever, he and Ira Sullivan organized a critically and commercially successful post-bop quintet. *Charlie Parker: The Verve Years (1950–51)* (Verve), *Modern Music from Chicago* (Fantasy), *The Red Arrow* (Onyx), *Night and Day* (Muse).

VERNEL FOURNIER

In 1958 Vernel Fournier created one of the most famous of all drum vamps — the understated, polyrhythmic figure that sets the stage for Ahmad Jamal's immensely popular rendition of "Poinciana." Fournier was an integral part of Jamal's trio for six years (1956–1962), demonstrating a firm pulse, subtle configurations, and a thorough grasp of dynamics. His stirring beat is traceable to the parade drumming he studied in New Orleans, where he was born in 1928. A professional from age 13, he made his name in Chicago in the early 1950s, eventually landing a spot in the Bee Hive's house band. After touring with George Shearing for two years and Jamal for another two, he settled in Chicago. But in the 1970s he moved to New York, where his sturdy beat has continued to benefit numerous musicians and singers. *Ahmad Jamal: But Not for Me* (Argo), *Ahmad Jamal: Poinciana* (Cadet), *George Shearing: Jazz Moments* (Capitol), *Benny Powell: Coast to Coast* (Trident).

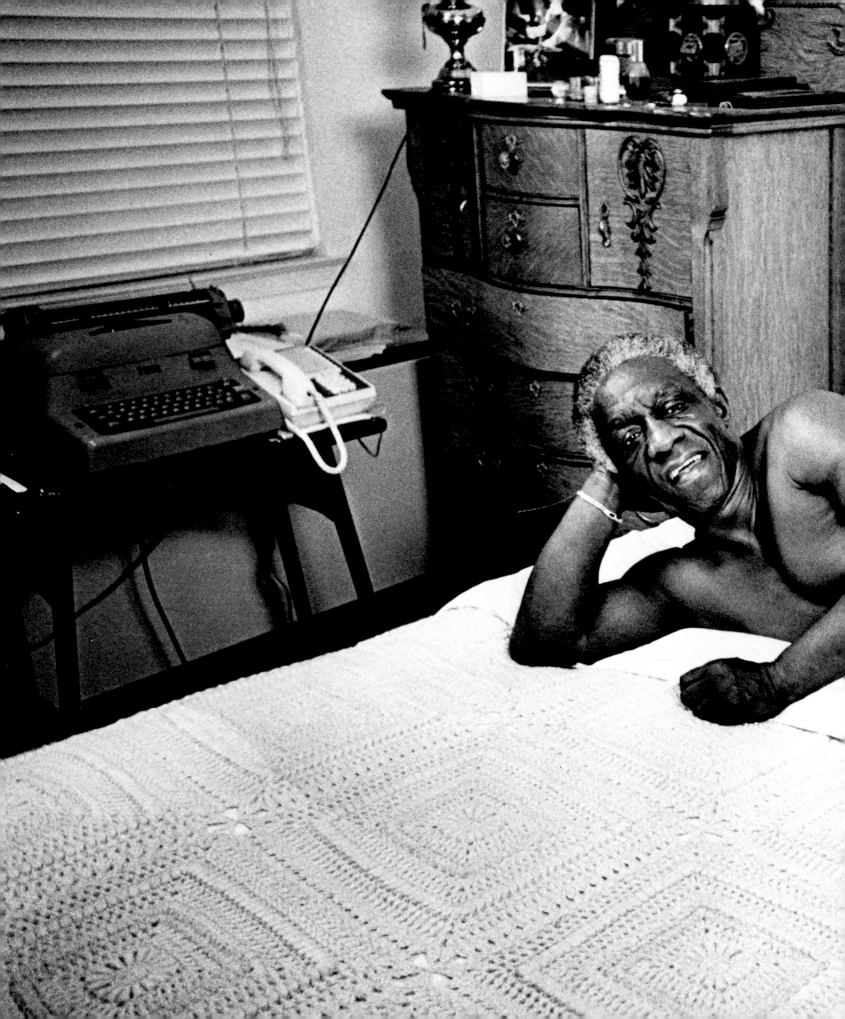

◄ ART BLAKEY

On one of his many classic albums, Art Blakey announces, "Yessir, I'm going to stay with the youngsters—it keeps the mind active." He ought to know. Blakey's band, the Jazz Messengers, is one of the most prestigious universities in jazz. Since organizing the group in 1947, the veteran drummer of big bands and bebop has played papa, professor, and preacher to a legion of renowned musicians, from Clifford Brown to Wynton Marsalis, from Horace Silver to Joanne Brackeen. The standard-bearer for a hard-driving style of music, Blakey is an apostle of jazz basics: muscular rhythms, functional themes, expressive clarity, and expansive improvisation. As a drummer, he is best known for his energetic swinging, vigorous press rolls, and razor-sharp responses to soloists. He is widely conceded to have been the ideal percussionist for Thelonious Monk. Born in Pittsburgh in 1919, Blakey has nurtured not only leading soloists, but musicians who subsequently became influential leaders in their own right. Small wonder; only the sturdiest souls can withstand the constant champing, goading, roaring, and rolling of his exuberant drums. *A Night at Birdland* (Blue Note), *Art Blakey's Jazz Messengers with Thelonious Monk* (Atlantic), *Moanin'* (Blue Note) *Album of the Year* (Timeless).

HILTON RUIZ

The prodigious Hilton Ruiz was born in New York City in 1952 and debuted at Carnegie Recital Hall eight years later. Trained in classical, jazz, and Latin idioms, he managed to combine diverse influences in excitingly rhythmic improvisations that employ parallel phrasing, advanced harmonies, and traditional jazz styles such as stride and boogie woogie. With such tutors as Mary Lou Williams and Rahsaan Roland Kirk encouraging him to learn the entire jazz tradition, he developed a remarkably broad repertory. Ruiz worked with several prominent musicians including Jackie McLean, Roy Haynes, Clark Terry, Roy Brooks, and Frank Foster, before joining Kirk's band in 1973. Since Kirk's death, Hilton has led a variety of groups and has steadily refined his technique. *Rahsaan Roland Kirk: Kirkatron* (Warners), *Piano Man* (SteepleChase), *Excitation* (SteepleChase).

◄ CEDAR WALTON

When Cedar Walton served as house pianist for Prestige Records in the 1960s, his richly intoned playing enhanced numerous sessions – sometimes to the point of stealing the spotlight from the leader. His consistency surprised some listeners, but not those who had followed his progress with J.J. Johnson (1958–1960), the Jazztet (1960–1961), and Art Blakey (1961–1964); they recognized in Walton a sensitive accompanist and a melodically fanciful soloist who makes every note count. Born in Dallas in 1934 to a piano teacher schooled in local rhythm and blues bands, he displayed a distinctive keyboard touch – firm and ringing – from the moment he arrived in New York. Through long associations with such musicians as Clifford Jordan, Billy Higgins, and the late Sam Jones, Cedar came to lead a series of trios and quartets noted for their warmth and precision, as well as for the high quality of Walton's original compositions. *J.J. Johnson: J.J. Inc.* (Columbia), *Cedar* (Prestige), *A Night at Boomers* (Muse), *Piano Solos* (Clean Cuts).

BUSTER WILLIAMS

Charles Anthony "Buster" Williams, Jr., was born in Camden, New Jersey, in 1942, but it was on the West Coast that he made his reputation. Playing with Nancy Wilson and the Jazz Crusaders in the mid-1960s, he was so widely talked about that visiting bandleaders would sometimes leave their bassists at home and use Buster as a sub. After touring with the Harold Land-Bobby Hutcherson Quintet and Herbie Hancock's Mwandishi, he settled in New York, where he is in constant demand for jazz gigs, studio work, and teaching assignments (he's affiliated with the Jazzmobile Workshop). As a member of Ron Carter's Piccolo Quartet, Williams developed a lasting alliance with Kenny Barron and Ben Riley that culminated in the 1982 debut of Sphere, a band dedicated to the music of Thelonious Monk. Known for his warm, fat sound and glissandos, he's also an accomplished composer. *Harold Land: The Peace-Maker* (Cadet), *Jimmy Rowles: The Peacocks* (Columbia), *Pinnacle* (Muse), *Heartbeat* (Muse).

BILLY HIGGINS

Born in Los Angeles in 1936, drummer Billy Higgins served an apprenticeship with rhythm and blues bands before hooking up with Ornette Coleman in 1958. The following year he traveled to New York with Coleman to play their historic engagement at the Five Spot. Despite his association with free jazz, Higgins won the admiration of jazzmen of various schools for his ability to swing hard while maintaining a light touch. His steady yet flexible time-keeping, unmistakable in its finesse, economy, and good humor, was heard on recordings with Dexter Gordon, Lee Morgan, Herbie Hancock, Sonny Rollins, and many others. In the 1970s he continued to record in various contexts. He has reunited several times with Coleman, and also formed a lasting association with Cedar Walton. *Ornette Coleman: Change of the Century* (Atlantic), *Lee Morgan: The Sidewinder* (Blue Note), *Jimmy Raney: The Influence* (Xanadu), *Cedar Walton: The Maestro* (Muse).

◄ ZOOT SIMS

John Haley "Zoot" Sims, a charter member of the Four Brothers school of Lester Young-inspired tenor saxophonists, has long since evolved into a classic stylist in his own right. His harmonic scope was shaped by the bop innovators, but he can swing with indomitable conviction and unmistakable warmth in any setting. Born in California in 1925, Zoot was on the road with big bands in his mid-teens. In addition to touring with Benny Goodman, Woody Herman, Gerry Mulligan, and Stan Kenton, he recorded with Clifford Brown and Miles Davis and made, under his own name, the first long-playing record for Prestige. In the 1950s he doubled on alto and baritone (occasionally over-dubbing ensemble passages on his records), and in the 1970s he added soprano. His notable long-term associations include Al Cohn (since 1957), Joe Venuti, and Jimmy Rowles. *Zootcase* (Prestige), *Joe and Zoot* (Chiaroscuro), *Basie and Zoot* (Pablo), *If I'm Lucky* (Pablo).

RANDY WESTON

Although he came to maturity at a time when most jazz pianists were under the dazzling spell of Bud Powell, Randy Weston found his own path in the ringing chords, angular dissonances, and thematic procedures of Duke Ellington and Thelonious Monk. Born in Brooklyn in 1924, Weston was encouraged to follow a career in music by some of the customers—including Charlie Parker—who frequented a restaurant he operated. His 1954 recording debut demonstrated his abilities as a composer as well; several of his tunes are now jazz standards. A school unto himself, he began using dancers in his performances in the late 1950s, and after his first tour of Africa in 1961, his music began to reflect an insightful African influence. In 1968 he settled in Tangier, where he opened a nightclub. Weston's music combines a strong, churning rhythmic base with folk melodies and exotic harmonies. His declamatory chords in the lower registers of the piano are like thunderclaps. *Zulu* (Milestone), *African Cookbook* (Atlantic), *Tanjah* (Polydor), *Blues to Africa* (Freedom).

JIM HALL

Jim Hall, one of the subtlest of jazz guitarists, was born in Buffalo, New York, in 1930, and educated at the Cleveland Institute of Music. Upon moving to Los Angeles in 1955, he joined the Chico Hamilton Quintet, the first in a series of wide-ranging associations that found him playing every kind of jazz and jazz-related music, from the Dukes of Dixieland to Gunther Schuller's Third Stream. He was especially memorable in the Sonny Rollins Quartet, the Jimmy Guiffre Trio, the Art Farmer Quartet, and in duets with Bill Evans and Lee Konitz. In every situation, his trim yet burnished tone added a warm glow to the ensemble, and his improvisations were economical and melodically adventurous. After a few years' residency on the Merv Griffin show, he began appearing in concert either with a trio or in duet with his favorite bassists, notably Ron Carter, Red Mitchell, and Don Thompson. *Sonny Rollins: The Bridge* (RCA), *Bill Evans: Interplay* (United Artists), *Commitment* (Horizon), *Circles* (Concord Jazz).

ARCHIE SHEPP

In the 1960s Archie Shepp sometimes seemed to arouse more controversy
with his forceful comments on the relationship between jazz and a hostile society
than with the equally forceful originality of his music. Yet his influence on the
avant-garde has been lasting: as a composer, he combined traditional and modernist
jazz styles with folk tunes, marches, and Tin Pan Alley baubles; as a saxophonist
(tenor and soprano), he revived sonorities and embouchure techniques that had
lain dormant since the advent of bop. Born in Florida in 1937 and raised in
Philadelphia, Shepp first came to prominence playing with Cecil Taylor, Bill Dixon,
and the New York Contemporary Five. Sponsored by John Coltrane, he recorded
a diverse series of albums that employed ambitious arrangements, African
influences, and the spoken word. His solos were either terse and pungent or
of marathon length and wildly energetic; more recent recordings are often
highlighted by his sensuous interpretations of ballads. Shepp has also written
plays, poetry, and essays, and since 1975 he has taught at the University of
Massachusetts in Amherst. *Four for Trane* (Impulse), *Fire Music* (Impulse), *Things
Have Got to Change* (Impulse), *Looking at Bird* (SteepleChase).

MARIAN McPARTLAND

Marian McPartland is one of jazz's most vibrant personalities. When she isn't making her points at the piano, she functions just as deftly as a journalist, radio personality, record producer (she owns the Halcyon label), consultant, and educator. Her wit and candor make her an irresistible spokeswoman, especially on a theme of particular importance to her: the role of women in jazz. Born Marian Turner in Windsor, England, in 1920, she met and married cornetist Jimmy McPartland during an army USO tour. For five years beginning in 1946, she worked in McPartland's band, but in 1951 she brought her own successful trio to New York's Hickory House. A sensitive interpreter of ballads, she was a favorite pianist of Alec Wilder, who composed 20 pieces for her. Her originals have been widely performed, and she remains a staple of New York's nightlife. *At the Hickory House* (Savoy), *The Music of Alec Wilder* (Halcyon), *Now's the Time* (Halcyon), *Portrait* (Concord Jazz).

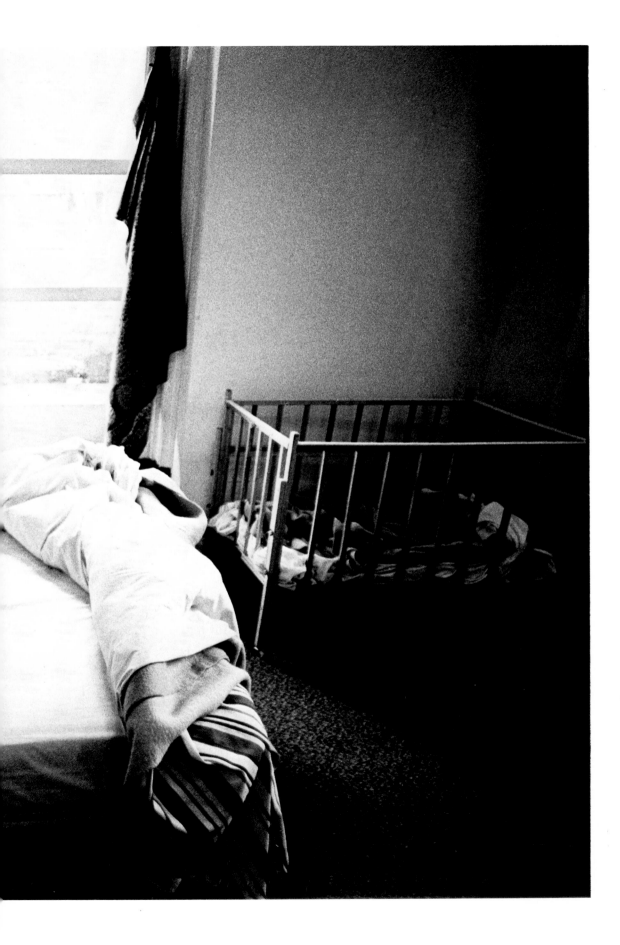

DEXTER GORDON

VIC DICKENSON

Few musicians are more widely admired than Vic Dickenson, the craftiest of
jazz trombonists. Famed for the sly, hang-dog sound he creates with an endless
variety of mutes (including a napkin, a hat, or if nothing else is available, his hand),
his elegant manipulation of the slide, and the droll irreverence with which
he consistently punctures Tin Pan Alley's most precious baubles, Dickenson is one
of the great dependables. He was born in Xenia, Ohio, in 1906, and worked with
several territory bands before achieving national prominence with the bands of
Claude Hopkins, Benny Carter, and Count Basie. His collaborations in the 1940s
with Sidney Bechet marked him as a traditionalist, but he was at home in any
context — playing the blues with Lester Young, boogie woogie with Albert
Ammons, or his own pretty ballads with Bobby Hackett. His work with Hackett in
the late 1960s led to a resurgence in his popularity, culminating in his joining the
World's Greatest Jazz Band. Dickenson is a subtly humorous trombonist, a
diverting singer, and a thoughtful composer, and his presence at a jam session is
virtually a guarantee of expressive, knowing jazz. *Lester Young: The Aladdin
Sessions* (Blue Note), *The Essential Vic Dickenson* (Vanguard), *Bobby Hackett: Live
at the Roosevelt Grill* (Chiaroscuro), *Vic Dickenson's Quintet* (Storyville).

CHET BAKER

Chet Baker was jazz's fair-haired boy in the cool 1950s. He was gifted, handsome, introverted, and sullen. Born in 1929 and raised in Oklahoma and California, he jammed with Charlie Parker in 1952, and became world famous a year later in Gerry Mulligan's pianoless quartet. Baker's trumpet had a thin, pale tone, but he made it reflect his moods with an intense, if restrained, passion. This shy intensity also characterized his style as a singer. Often compared with Miles Davis in the early years, he soon blossomed into a genuine melodist in his own right. Then came the much publicized bouts with narcotics, and the arrests. After a long hiatus, he returned to music. His sound is richer and more powerful now, and his lyricism is still tender and affecting. *Gerry Mulligan/Lee Konitz: Revelation* (Blue Note), *Chet Baker in New York* (Riverside), *She Was Too Good to Me* (CTI), *The Touch of Your Lips* (SteepleChase).

JIMMY HEATH

Born in 1926, Jimmy Heath was touring with carnivals while still in his teens. By the late 1940s he was leading a legendary orchestra in his native Philadelphia (the neighborhood recruits included John Coltrane, Benny Golson, and Johnny Coles). When he first came to New York, musicians called him Little Bird because he was small and played alto like Charlie Parker. In 1953 he switched to tenor sax and recorded one of his first compositions, "C.T.A.," with Miles Davis and the All-Stars. During the following decade he clinched his reputation as a first-rate saxophonist and as the composer of lively, ingeniously crafted compositions that other musicians enjoyed playing. His saxophone style combines high-speed lyricism and driving riffs; his tone is weighty and sure. As a composer-arranger, he has achieved new maturity in the 1970s with his (unrecorded) *Afro-American Suite of Evolution*, and with his settings for the marvelous band he organized with Albert and Percy, the Heath Brothers. *Fast Company* (Milestone), *The Gap Sealer* (Cobblestone), *Picture of Heath* (Xanadu), *Brotherly Love* (Antilles).

PERCY HEATH

Trained originally on violin, Percy Heath began studying bass when he was discharged from the Air Corps (he was a fighter pilot in World War II). Six months later, he was playing professionally. In 1947 Howard McGhee brought him to New York, where he immediately made his mark as one of the outstanding bassists of the era. Widely noted for his superb time, taste, and intonation, he participated in seminal recordings with Dizzy Gillespie, Charlie Parker, Theolonious Monk, and Miles Davis. Born in Philadelphia in 1923, Heath is best known for his 22 years with the Modern Jazz Quartet, which he helped form in 1952. He appeared a rather retiring figure during that period, yet when he organized the Heath Brothers with his brothers Jimmy and Albert in the 1970s, he emerged as a bandstand wit as well as a clever composer. His solos, often played on baby bass (which combines a cello body with bass tuning), are intensely rhythmic and technically perfect. He now has two ideal forums for his talent—the ongoing Heath Brothers and the reunited Modern Jazz Quartet. *Miles Davis: Tune Up* (Prestige), *The Modern Jazz Quartet: The Last Concert* (Atlantic), *Passing Thru* (Columbia), *In Motion* (Columbia).

◄ JOE WILLIAMS

Born in Cordele, Georgia, in 1918, Joe Williams was raised in Chicago, where he made his professional singing debut at 19 with Jimmie Noone. For more than 15 years he remained a local attraction. That changed on Christmas day, 1954, when Count Basie hired him. Within months, their recording of "Every Day" brought Williams to international attention, and catapulted Basie into his period of greatest popularity. Williams went on his own in 1961, though his reunion appearances with Basie—they refer to each other as father and son—have been numerous. A six-foot-one baritone with three octaves, impeccable timing, and a finely honed sense of drama, he is equally convincing with blues or ballads. Williams lives in Las Vegas but works everywhere, and when the spirit hits him he can whip an audience into a frenzy. His colleagues admire him as much for his professionalism as his talent, and although he is one of the great jazz singers, he records all too rarely. *Count Basie Swings/Joe Williams Sings* (Verve), *At Newport '63* (RCA), *Presenting Joe Williams and Thad Jones–Mel Lewis* (Solid State), *Live* (Fantasy).

GEORGE SHEARING

George Shearing was born in 1919 in London, where he studied classical music until, at 16, he began to listen to recordings by Teddy Wilson, Art Tatum, and other American jazz pianists. He was soon playing piano in an all-blind dance band, making his recording debut at 19. A post-war visit established him in the United States and in 1949 he organized the quintet that would make him world famous. Noted for its cool unison phrasing of piano, guitar, and vibes, the elegant virtuosity of Shearing's block chords (an extension of the locked-hands style of piano playing originated by Milt Buckner), and the inclusion after 1954 of Latin percussion, the group was enormously popular until it disbanded in 1962. Shearing enjoyed additional success as the composer of "Conception" and the ubiquitous "Lullaby of Birdland." In recent years he has frequently performed unaccompanied as well as with duos, trios, and symphony orchestras. *So Rare* (Savoy), *Touch of Genius* (MGM), *500 Miles High* (MPS), *George Shearing/Jim Hall: First Edition* (Concord Jazz).

JAY McSHANN

Born in Muskogee, Oklahoma, in 1916, Jay McShann first passed through Kansas City in the 1930s, and was soon in demand as a hard-driving blues pianist. By 1941 he was at the helm of the last of the great territory bands; it introduced the solo style of a young saxophonist named Charlie Parker and achieved commercial success with such juke joint favorites as "Confessing the Blues" and "Hootie Blues." Unfortunately, the presence of Parker and of vocalist Walter Brown completely overshadowed the talents of the leader. Only since 1969, when McShann made a triumphant tour of Europe, was he widely recognized as an incisive pianist with a repertoire that encompassed Fats Waller and Thelonious Monk as well as the barrelhouse tradition. He can be exhilarating at impromptu sessions, adding tremendous vitality to rhythm sections and inspiring soloists. He also developed into a convincing singer of blues and ballads. McShann continues to make his home in Kansas City, and tours frequently, often teaming up with such territory veterans as violinist Claude Williams, saxophonist Buddy Tate, and singer Joe Turner. *Jay McShann 1941–1943* (MCA), *Jimmy Witherspoon: Goin' to Kansas City Blues* (RCA), *The Man from Muskogee* (Sackville), *The Last of the Blue Devils* (Atlantic).

TOMMY FLANAGAN

A musician's musician, the professorial Tommy Flanagan was born in Detroit in 1930, and debuted at age 15 with Dexter Gordon. After arriving in New York, his piano playing was heard on countless recording sessions in the 1950s, including major albums by Sonny Rollins, Miles Davis, Wes Montgomery, and John Coltrane. Nor was he confined to modern jazz; he was a favorite of several mainstream musicians, especially Coleman Hawkins. He was also recognized as a nonpareil accompanist for singers; he toured with Tony Bennett for a year and with Ella Fitzgerald for 10. Dynamic and sure, incapable of bad taste, Flanagan can be a spellbinder. Yet it wasn't until the mid-1970s that he emerged as a lucid, compelling stylist with an unusually extensive repertoire. Flanagan has since recorded a series of duo and trio albums that demonstrate the versatility of bop piano and confirm his place as one of the most authoritative pianists of his generation. *Trio and Sextet* (Onyx), *Eclypso* (Inner City), *Montreux '77* (Pablo), *Giant Steps* (Enja).

BARRY HARRIS

Barry Harris is almost as well known for his stubborn integrity as for the subtle complexities and beauties of his piano style. His unshaken allegiance to the tradition of Parker, Powell, and Monk has made him a premiere custodian of bop. He was a local legend in the 1950s, when such musicians as Miles Davis, Lester Young, and Max Roach passed through Detroit, where he was born in 1929, and returned to New York singing his praises. In 1960 Cannonball Adderley persuaded Harris to come East to join his quintet; associations with Yusef Lateef and Coleman Hawkins followed. Fastidious and dependable, he was at the keyboard when a number of musicians recorded their finest work. In addition to his achievements as a pianist, composer, and arranger, Harris has an impressive record as a teacher; several of his students participate in the highly ambitious annual New York concert he's given since 1980, combining jazz musicians, strings, dancers, and singers. In 1982 he opened his own nightclub, the Jazz Cultural Theater, in New York. *Stay Right With It* (Milestone), *Luminescence!* (Prestige), *Live in Tokyo* (Xanadu), *Barry Harris Plays Barry Harris* (Xanadu).

94

SADIK HAKIM

Argonne Dense Thornton was working in a Chicago club when Charlie Parker walked in, unpacked his horn, and started wailing with the band. Five years later, Parker invited him to play piano on his first session as a leader. Two years after that, Thornton converted to Islam, adopting the name by which he became known—Sadik Hakim. Born in Duluth, Minnesota, in 1919, Hakim performed with swing and bop players; he accompanied Lester Young (Hakim is the composer of "Jumping with Symphony Sid"), Ben Webster, Dexter Gordon, and James Moody. After touring with several bands and leading his own trio, he moved to Canada for more than a decade. When he returned to New York in 1976, he resumed recording and touring, developing a large following in Japan. Employing the same idiosyncratic piano style he first unveiled with Parker, he continued to work in New York until his death in 1983. *Charlie Parker: The Master Takes* (Savoy), *Lester Young: The Complete Aladdins* (Blue Note), *I Remember Bebop* (Columbia), *Sonny Stitt Meets Sadik Hakim* (Progressive).

HERBIE HANCOCK

Born in Chicago in 1940, Herbie Hancock started piano lessons at age seven, and four years later played Mozart with the Chicago Symphony. He was studying engineering in college when Donald Byrd took him on tour, and in no time he was entrenched in the New York scene. One of his earliest compositions, "Watermelon Man," was a big hit for Mongo Santamaria. In 1963 Miles Davis made him the pilot of the most celebrated rhythm section of the decade; for five years, Hancock's evocative chords, modal improvising, and blues feeling were essential to the Davis quintet. At the same time he recorded a series of albums under his own name, served as a sideman on numerous sessions, composed jingles, and scored the film *Blow-Up*. After leaving Davis, Hancock organized a sextet that reflected his increasing interest in electronics, and after moving to Los Angeles in 1972, he achieved tremendous popularity with a new band that specialized in a jocular brand of funk. In recent years, he has occasionally returned to acoustic music—notably in duets with Chick Corea and with the V.S.O.P. Quintet. *Takin' Off* (Blue Note), *Miles Davis: My Funny Valentine* (Columbia), *Empyrean Isles* (Blue Note), *V.S.O.P. The Quintet* (Columbia).

THAD JONES

MEL LEWIS

In the tradition of such timekeeping colorists as Jo Jones, Chick Webb, and Tiny Kahn, Mel Lewis is a stylist of big band drumming—a musician who keeps the machinery of an orchestra rolling smoothly without recourse to pyrotechnics. Born in Buffalo in 1929, the son of a professional drummer, Lewis played with a variety of bands before turning 20. After two years with Stan Kenton (1954–1956), he settled in Los Angeles, where he organized a quintet with Bill Holman, handled a variety of studio assignments, and joined Terry Gibbs's big band. Back in New York in the 1960s, he worked regularly with Gerry Mulligan and Dizzy Gillespie. Then in 1965 he and Thad Jones established the Jazz Orchestra as a Monday night feature at the Village Vanguard. Dozens of talented musicians passed through its ranks, and though Jones left it in 1979, Lewis keeps it going as the most durable orchestra of its era. *Jazz for a Sunday Afternoon* (Solid State), *Consummation* (Blue Note), *Mel Lewis and Friends* (Horizon), *Live in Montreux* (Pausa).

CLARK TERRY

Not since Fats Waller has there been so persistently ebullient a jazz personality as Clark Terry. Born in St. Louis in 1920, Terry apprenticed with various bands, including those of Lionel Hampton, Charlie Barnet, and Eddie Cleanhead Vinson, before attracting national attention with Count Basie's octet. In 1951 he embarked on an eight-year stint with Duke Ellington and matured into an instantly recognizable trumpet stylist, combining a witty, puckish sound with breathtaking facility. Although he spent most of the 1960s with the NBC studio orchestra, he also found time to co-lead a quintet with Bob Brookmeyer, and to debut, on an Oscar Peterson record, his alter ego Mumbles, the "method" blues singer. When he isn't touring college campuses as a clinician, Terry occasionally appears with his own excellent big band or quintet. A favorite gambit is his ability to play duets with himself—trumpet in right hand, flugelhorn in left. *Cruising* (Milestone), *Oscar Peterson Trio Plus One* (Mercury), *Montreux '77: the Jam Sessions* (Pablo), *Memories of Duke* (Pablo).

JOANNE BRACKEEN

The indefatigable Joanne Brackeen was born in Ventura, California in 1938. Although she was playing piano professionally at age 20, marriage and four children in quick succession eclipsed her career for more than a decade. Then, during a period in which she appeared with a number of important bandleaders, including Art Blakey, Joe Henderson, and Stan Getz, she developed an intense, even furious style that belied the owlish passivity of her appearance, and attracted the interest of several record labels. Like McCoy Tyner, whose influence she assimilated and personalized, Brackeen combined a powerful touch with an architectonic approach, demonstrating digital precision, emotional force, and a highly developed sense of form. Heard frequently in piano-bass duets around New York, she is a prolific composer of complex piano pieces, and probably the most accomplished woman instrumentalist in jazz since Mary Lou Williams. *Snooze* (Choice), *Mythical Magic* (Pausa), *Special Identity* (Antilles).

CHARLES MINGUS

The uncompromising, occasionally ornery, always outspoken Charles Mingus was an explosive force in jazz for nearly 40 years. Drawing on the music of Ellington, Tatum, Parker, and the church, he created a compositional style of his own, the impact of which is readily apparent throughout the jazz world of the 1980s. He is considered by many to have been the premier bassist of his time, noted for his extraordinay technical facility and stirring emotional power. Yet Mingus himself always insisted that he never achieved his full potential as an instrumentalist because of the time he devoted to composing for and leading the series of bands he called the Jazz Workshop. Mingus was born in Arizona in 1922, and raised in Los Angeles, where he worked with Louis Armstrong and Lionel Hampton (who recorded his seminal "Mingus Fingers"). After arriving in New York in 1951, he participated in the legendary bebop concert at Massey Hall, and toured with the Red Norvo trio. But Mingus was already composing extended works that combined traditional and avant-garde techniques. Under his leadership, several major musicians—including Eric Dolphy, Rahssan Roland Kirk, Booker Ervin, Ted Curson, and Jaki Byard—first realized their own capabilities. He composed for and conducted his final record sessions from a wheelchair, his awesome spirit seemingly undaunted by the degenerative disease that took his life in 1979. *Passions of a Man* (Atlantic), *Mingus Presents Mingus* (Candid), *Great Moments* (MCA Impulse), *Let My Children Hear Music* (Columbia).

RAHSAAN ROLAND KIRK

Rahsaan Roland Kirk was one of the miracle men of contemporary music. Born in Columbus, Ohio, in 1936, he was educated at the Ohio School of the Blind and organized his own band at 15. After a dream in which he blew several horns simultaneously, he taught himself to play two extinct members of the saxophone family (the soprano-like manzello and the alto-like stritch) at the same time that he played tenor. Not only did he manage to propel all three horns with stunning power, but he contrived imaginative parallel harmonies, contrapuntal melodies, and stop-time effects. He also played dozens of flutes and percussion instruments, composed memorable melodies, sang, and strongly encouraged numerous young musicians to master the entire jazz tradition. He would have been an imposing figure had he done nothing but play tenor sax—his mastery of circular breathing techniques was matchless and his speed stupefying. After a crippling stroke, he invented a fingering box that allowed him to play with one hand. He died in 1978. *We Free Kings* (Mercury), *Rip, Rig and Panic* (Limelight), *The Jaki Byard Experience* (Prestige), *Bright Moments* (Atlantic).

DIZZY GILLESPIE

As a trumpeter, composer, arranger, and bandleader, the ageless John Birks Gillespie has been an innovator in every facet of jazz. Born in Cheraw, South Carolina, in 1917, he arrived in Philadelphia in the mid-1930s, replacing his idol Roy Eldridge in the Teddy Hill orchestra and earning the nickname Dizzy for his shenanigans on and off the stage. He soloed memorably and wrote several arrangements for Cab Calloway, but by 1941 he was moving away from the Eldridge style in favor of something entirely new in jazz trumpet. Woodshedding in New York with Charlie Parker, Thelonious Monk, and a few others, Gillespie was beginning to define the aesthetics of modern jazz—the so-called bebop style. His flashy yet expressively balanced improvisations were characterized by thrilling arpeggios of breathtaking length, rhythmic unpredictability, dynamics, high-note shouts, and harmonic daring. In 1946 he created a virtuoso big band that experimented with modality, popularized Afro-Cuban rhythms, and served as a training camp for numerous players and composers. In recent years Gillespie has become an increasingly expressive player and a more convincing bluesman. For more than 40 years his gifts as comic, singer, dancer, and percussionist have been ancillary to his genius as a trumpeter in displaying the highly accessible beauty and excitement of his music. And the *enfant terrible* is *still* on the road. *The Development of an American Artist* (Smithsonian), *The Greatest of Dizzy Gillespie* (RCA), *Have Trumpet, Will Excite* (Verve), *The Gifted Ones* (Pablo).

JON FADDIS

Jon Faddis of Oakland, California, made his New York reputation overnight when he subbed for an ailing Roy Eldridge at a 1972 Charles Mingus concert. The next morning, everyone was talking about this nineteen-year-old trumpeter who could play like Dizzy Gillespie. Faddis had been introduced to Dizzy's music only four years earlier, but he quickly mastered the strenuous difficulties of his idol's style, imbuing it with a fire all his own. He also revealed Dizzyisms in his bandstand behavior, which could be wry, prankish, and just plain naughty. His extraordinary technique—which included cloudless high notes that reflect the influence of Snooky Young—enabled him to become a prolific studio man, but he continues to appear on the bandstand whenever Gillespie performs in New York, and in 1983 he organized his own quintet. *Mingus and Friends* (Columbia), *Young Blood* (Pablo), *Dizzy Gillespie: Montreux '77* (Pablo).

SY OLIVER

Sy Oliver was born in Battle Creek, Michigan, in 1910, the son of two music teachers who provided him with a foundation in arranging, trumpet playing, and singing. After an apprenticeship with territory bands, Oliver submitted arrangements to Jimmie Lunceford, who recruited him in 1933. During the next few years, Oliver perfected a unique style of writing in which a variety of ideas and techniques were marshaled into surprising juxtapositions and parsed over a constant two-beat rhythmic base. His muted trumpet solos were patterned after those of Bubber Miley and his singing was light and appealing, but it was his witty arrangements that had the most impact. In 1939 Tommy Dorsey hired Oliver away from Lunceford, thereby transfiguring the Dorsey orchestra. In later years Oliver became a prolific freelance arranger, a music director for the New York Jazz Repertory Company, and a record producer. His small, tightly-knit dance band has continued to perform in the 1980s. *Jimmie Lunceford: Harlem Shout* (MCA), *Jimmie Lunceford: For Dancers Only* (MCA), *The Best of Tommy Dorsey* (RCA), *Frank Sinatra: I Remember Tommy* (Reprise).

BOB BROOKMEYER

For most of his career, Bob Brookmeyer was best known as a valve trombonist with a style that combined ironic wit and a curious brand of rural lyricism. In recent years his improvisational gifts have taken a back seat to his composing and arranging. Born in Kansas City in 1929, Brookmeyer began writing for local bands at 14, and came to New York in 1952. A series of memorable collaborations ensued, including those with Stan Getz, Jimmy Guiffre, and Gerry Mulligan, and an anomalous album of piano duets with Bill Evans. With Clark Terry he organized a brightly swinging, occasionally whimsical quintet in the early 1960s. Later in the decade he performed, composed, and arranged for the Thad Jones–Mel Lewis Jazz Orchestra. Brookmeyer retreated into the California studios for most of the 1970s, emerging in the 1980s as the musical director for the Mel Lewis Orchestra. *Presenting the Gerry Mulligan Sextet* (Mercury), *Tonight* (Mainstream), *Bob Brookmeyer and Friends* (Columbia), *Mel Lewis: New Works by Bob Brookmeyer* (Finesse).

ROY ELDRIDGE

For nearly 50 years, Roy Eldridge has been one of the most exhilarating soloists in jazz. No one has better exemplified the love of playing, or worked harder to maintain a personal standard of excellence. Born in Pittsburgh in 1911, he played drums before turning his attention to the trumpet, and soon picked up the sobriquet "Little Jazz" because fellow musicians recognized in him the very embodiment of the music's energy, spontaneity, and fire. In the 1930s he led a thrilling band at Chicago's Three Deuces, performed with Fletcher Henderson, and recorded a series of solos that firmly established him as the seminal jazz trumpeter after Louis Armstrong, as well as the man who paved the way for Dizzy Gillespie. The 1940s found him handsomely featured as the star soloist with Gene Krupa's band, and later with Artie Shaw's. It was with Krupa (for whom he occasionally substituted on drums) that he recorded the immortal "Rockin' Chair," developed his talents as a singer-entertainer, and broke the Jim Crow rule that prevented a black musician from playing in a white band. Roy never played it safe or easy, even after 1970, when he began a 10-year stand at New York's Jimmy Ryan's. *The Early Years* (Columbia), *Little David the Goliath* (MCA), *Dale's Wail* (Verve), *The Nifty Cat* (MJR).

SARAH VAUGHAN

There may be singers who can rival Sarah Vaughan's voice and range, her improvisational inventiveness, or her passion and feeling, but no one else can do it all. Born in Newark, New Jersey, in 1924, she sang in church and studied piano before winning the amateur contest that led to a job with Earl Hines. Vaughan was immediately taken up by the young modernists, and recorded with Charlie Parker, Dizzy Gillespie, Tadd Dameron, and others. In the 1950s she managed to record uncompromising jazz albums (Clifford Brown and Miles Davis were among her accompanists) as well as a string of pop hits. Yet by the mid–1960s, her unflagging creativity displeased record producers who wanted to fit her into a commercial mold, and she refused to record for five years. Today, rather incredibly, her luscious voice, swelling and diminishing with utter control, high notes beaming like lasers and lows booming sonorously, is as rich as ever, and she records and performs as she pleases. *The Divine Sarah* (Musicraft), *Sarah Vaughan* (Trip), *Live in Japan* (Mainstream), *Gershwin Live!* (Columbia).

JIMMY ROWLES

Few members of the audience were familiar with Jimmy Rowles when he was billed as "California's greatest jazz pianist" at a Town Hall concert with Johnny Mercer in 1973, but by the end of the year he was firmly ensconced in New York's piano-bar circuit, where he remained a mainstay until hooking up with Zoot Sims's quartet in 1978. Born in Spokane, Washington, in 1918, Rowles worked with Woody Herman, Benny Goodman, and other bandleaders before earning a reputation as a singer's accompanist — an acknowledged favorite of Billie Holiday, Carmen McRae, Sarah Vaughan, Ella Fitzgerald, and others. Widely recognized as a master stylist for his startling lyricism, advanced harmonies, and subtle dynamics (including closed chords so deftly muted they sound as though he were wearing mittens), Rowles also writes lovely ballads and weird novelties, and sings them with an appealing croak. *Heavy Love* (Xanadu), *We Could Make Such Beautiful Music Together* (Xanadu), *Zoot Sims: I Wish I Were Twins* (Pablo), *Plays Duke Ellington and Billy Strayhorn* (Columbia).

EUBIE BLAKE

Few careers in all of music are more remarkable than that of centenarian James Hubert "Eubie" Blake. Born in Baltimore in 1883, he wrote the influential "Charleston Rag" at 16 and was soon playing piano in brothels, dancing with medicine shows, and touring in vaudeville. With his partner, the lyricist and singer Noble Sissle, he created one of the legendary theatrical successes of the 1920s, *Shuffle Along* (for which he composed "I'm Just Wild About Harry"). His most celebrated melody, "Memories of You," was written for *Blackbirds of 1930*. At 62 Eubie earned a degree in music from New York University, and fifteen years later proved, with a couple of records and concert appearances, that his powers at the keyboard (once lavishly praised by James P. Johnson) remained undiminished. Yet it wasn't until he recorded an extraordinary "comeback" album at 86 that he became an international celebrity, spurring a full-scale reinvestigation of his largely forgotten accomplishments. As pianist, singer, composer, and raconteur, Blake was the most vital living link between jazz and its precursors, and his humor, candor, and vitality made him a most cherished ambassador of American music. He died a few days after his 100th birthday. *Early Rare Recordings* (EBM), *The Wizard of Ragtime* (20th Century Fox), *The 86 Years of Eubie Blake* (Columbia), *From Rags to Classics* (EBM).

If you are playing jazz, you have to play what comes out at any moment—
something you never said before.

John Coltrane

ACKNOWLEDGMENTS

My father's choice record collection was my 52nd Street. This valuable listening foundation started it all.

My parents, Al and Linda Friedman, have been a great source of encouragement to me. Their continual admiration and support have helped tremendously in making this book possible.

Michele Singer, Jerry Wexler, John Snyder, and Lin Crouch were my supreme advisory committee. They put up with and encouraged my total obsession with this book and cheered me on for what felt like forever. Through every stage of production from beginning to end they were consultants, editors, hand-holders, fans, and assistants. I literally could not have completed this project without their love and inspiration.

I would like to thank Joseph D'Anna for his love, his humor, his belief in me, and his special understanding of my work.

I am very grateful to the following people for their invaluable assistance:

Sidney Rapoport, for his enormous contribution, his dedication to quality, and his rare generosity and character; Max Gordon for his kindness and encouragement, and for giving me free rein in The Vanguard, where I got so much of my inspiration; Carin Goldberg for her endless designing hours; Nina Murano for her wisdom, guidance, and friendship; Phoebe Jacobs for her constant help and research, and for introducing me to Eubie; Charles Traub for understanding the identity of this book before I did, and for steering me in all the right directions; Gary Giddins for his patience, talent, understanding, and generous collaboration; Maribeth Anderson Payne for making this book possible.

The jazz clubs, where many of my photographs were taken: The Village Vanguard, The Blue Note, Fat Tuesday's, Sweet Basil, Lush Life, Seventh Avenue South, Eddie Condon's, Bradley's, Marty's, The Bottom Line, and The Village Gate.

Special thanks to Charles E. Smith, Sean Callahan, Joan Greenfield, Mort Rosenberg, Gene Greif, Julie Connery, Milton Greene, Arnold Skolnick, David Turner, Peter Casenza, Barbara Daglion, George Dukas, Bruce Lundvall, Harry Whiting, Elliot Hoffman, Deirdre Murphy, Ornette Coleman, Diana Parker, Tad Yamashiro, Debbie Friedman, Michelle Toland, George Chinsee, John Hammond, Olivia Taylor, Janet Rogler, Quincy Jones, John Levy, Jim Gicking, Nat Hentoff, Cosmos, Maxine Gregg, Steve Getz, John Flateau, Willard Alexander, Laurie Pepper, Hank Jones, William B. Williams, Mona Heath, Donna Austin Ozzimo, Harry Addesso, and Nicky.

Portriga photographic paper was provided by the courtesy of Agfa Gevaert.

Photographic materials used in the completion of this book were provided by The Photo Exchange, New York.

INDEX

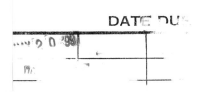